# ANYWHERE THAT IS

# WILD

## JOHN MUIR'S
## FIRST WALK TO YOSEMITE

*Edited by*
PETER & DONNA THOMAS

YOSEMITE CONSERVANCY
*Yosemite National Park*

When at last, stricken and faint like a crushed insect, you hope to escape from all the terrible grandeur of these mountain powers, other fountains, other oceans break forth before you; for there, in clear view, over heaps and rows of foothills, is laid a grand, smooth, outspread plain, watered by a river, and another range of peaky, snow-capped mountains a hundred miles in the distance. That plain is the valley of the San Joaquin, and those mountains are the great Sierra Nevada.

—JOHN MUIR, *A Thousand-Mile Walk to the Gulf*

# CONTENTS

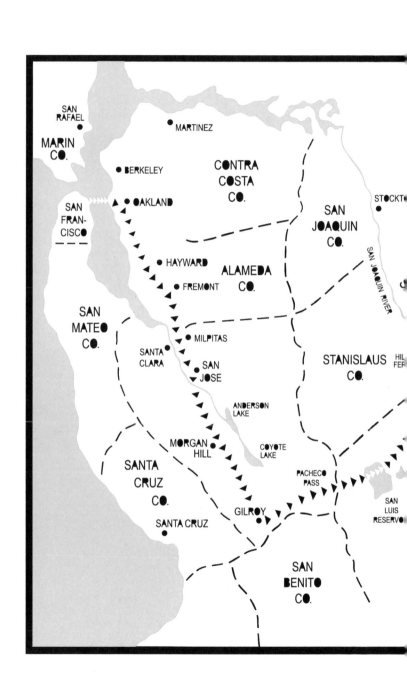

SAN
RAFAEL

MARIN
CO.

MARTINEZ

BERKELEY

CONTRA
COSTA
CO.

STOCKTO

OAKLAND

SAN
FRAN-
CISCO

SAN
JOAQUIN
CO.

SAN JOAQUIN RIVER

HAYWARD

ALAMEDA
CO.

FREMONT

SAN
MATEO
CO.

MILPITAS

SANTA
CLARA

SAN
JOSE

STANISLAUS
CO.

HIL
FER

ANDERSON
LAKE

MORGAN
HILL

COYOTE
LAKE

SANTA
CRUZ
CO.

PACHECO
PASS

SAN
LUIS
RESERVO

GILROY

SANTA CRUZ

SAN
BENITO
CO.

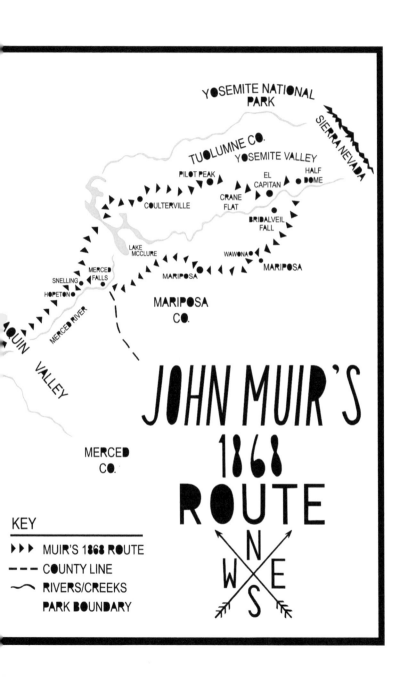

# PREFACE

WHAT FOLLOWS IS THE STORY of John Muir's 1868 walk across California from San Francisco to Yosemite. John Muir, noted naturalist, writer, and father of the worldwide conservation movement, was born in Scotland in 1838. His family immigrated to America in 1849 and settled near Portage, Wisconsin. Muir grew up as a hardworking farm boy with a deep, abiding love of nature. He proved to be an able inventor, creating machines composed of whittled cogs and levers to perform various semipractical operations, like a mechanism that connected a clock to his bed and tipped him out when it was time to rise. When he was twenty-two, he entered the University of Wisconsin, studying the natural sciences and intending to become a physician as a way to help humanity. Then, as part of his eclectic, self-directed education, Muir began to study botany. In the summer of 1863, he set off on his first long walk, accompanied by two fellow students; it was a botanical and geological tour down the Wisconsin River Valley and into Iowa. On completing this trip, Muir, instead of returning to school, set out on another walking trip, this time from Wisconsin to Canada, into what he called "the University of the Wilderness."

It is interesting to contemplate that John Muir might never have come to California to take *this* walk—and thus might never have been in the position to influence President Theodore Roosevelt to set aside Yosemite as a national park—if he hadn't first had an accident. In 1867, after returning home from his walk to Canada, Muir took a job in a wagon-wheel factory in Indianapolis and, while at work one day, pierced his right eye with an awl. Both eyes went blind. Muir, whose passion at this time was botany, vowed if he ever recovered his sight, he would not return to work on his mechanical inventions but would travel the world, and "devote the rest of my life to the study of the inventions of God."

Fortunately, his eyesight *did* return, and he set off soon after, walking from Indianapolis to the

Gulf of Mexico with the intention to go on to South America and find the source of the Amazon, where he would build a raft and float to the Atlantic. But Muir contracted malaria in Florida and changed his plans: "I decided to visit California for a year or two to see its wonderful flora and the famous Yosemite Valley. All the world was before me and every day was a holiday, so it did not seem important to which one of the world's wildernesses I first should wander."

## The Book Muir Did Not Write

John Muir wrote many books and articles during his lifetime. Some were autobiographical, some told tall tales of his adventures in the wilderness, and some shared his observations of nature. But he never wrote a book that told about his 1868 ramble across California to see Yosemite and the giant trees of the Mariposa Grove. When he was alive, it was not a story that would have interested many people. Back when there was still plenty of open space in California—when the roads were lined with natural beauty and walking along them was not so unsafe—people would have wanted to read of an epic adventure in the wilderness rather than a story about trying to *get* to the wilderness. But time has changed things; and now, if someone walks from San Francisco to Yosemite, it is a story worth telling. In fact, it is front-page news. We know that is true because it happened to us.

## Documenting Muir's Trip

In 2004, Donna was hiking the John Muir Trail—a 212-mile hiking route, named in Muir's honor, that travels along the crest of California's Sierra Nevada range from Yosemite Valley to Mount Whitney—when someone told this apocryphal story: "You know, John Muir would just grab a loaf of bread, put some tea in his pocket, throw a coat over his shoulder, walk right out his front door, and keep going till he got to Yosemite." Donna decided then and there that she was going to follow in Muir's footsteps and walk from Santa Cruz to Yosemite. When she got home, she asked if I wanted to join her, and I replied, "Let's find out what Muir did, and *do* what he did."

So we went to the Holt-Atherton Special Collections at the University of the Pacific (UOP) in Stockton, California, to look through the John Muir Papers to find what he had done. We searched long and hard but found no documentary evidence that Muir had ever walked from any of his homes to Yosemite. However, we *did* find that he had walked from San Francisco to Yosemite in April of 1868, when he first arrived in California. And that was what we were going to do.

To replicate Muir's journey, we needed to know exactly where he walked. His diary for the 1868 trip is missing, but we did find thirteen other sources—articles, books, and letters—in which John Muir wrote about the trip. Each was written for a different reason and so described the journey from a different perspective. For example, in the magazine article titled "Rambles of a Botanist," Muir focused on the flora, while in his book *The Yosemite*, he was concerned with the landscape. These sources gave us a rough outline of the route, but the details were all confused. We figured the only chance we had of understanding the whole story would be to combine all the accounts into a single narrative.

## Compiling This Narrative

To create the story that follows, we sorted Muir's writings by geographical region (e.g., San Francisco Bay Area, Pacheco Pass, San Joaquin Valley, etc.), and then we combined everything sentence by sentence. Duplicate passages were merged; word order and sentence structure were altered when necessary; case and tense were changed when they no longer matched; and, occasionally, a word was inserted for clarity. Our guiding rule was to change as little as possible. When we finished, the story was clear, and we felt we really did know what Muir had done. On April 1, 2006, we left from the San Francisco Ferry Building on our own 310-mile trans-California ramble.[1]

In 2010, the account of our travels was published along with the compiled text of Muir's story as *Muir Ramble Route: Walking from San Francisco to Yosemite in the Footsteps of John Muir*. Muir's story is written in the form of a letter—one that he might have written to a friend or family member shortly after finishing his own trip to Yosemite. In his letter, Muir first reflects on the trip as a whole, then gives the details, concluding with a plea to come visit California, saying, "Yosemite alone is worth the expense and danger of any journey in the world."

The source material for each paragraph can be found in the Source Notes starting on page 45 of this book. Where the text is from combined sources, the primary source is listed first, the secondary source listed next, and so on. Brackets indicate added information. For those interested in referring to our sources, John Muir's books can be found in most reference libraries. The additional materials, including his original letters and personal artifacts, are held in the archives at the University of the Pacific and the University of Wisconsin in Madison. As mentioned before, the collection at UOP holds the original journals for Muir's 1867 thousand-mile walk and his first summer in the Sierra, in 1869. But the journal for his 1868 trip across California is missing. Had it not been lost, or had Muir written a book about the trip, his 1868 journey to Yosemite would be better known today.

We hope that, with this telling, the story will become better known, and that it will inspire you— whether on foot, by bike, or by car—to follow Muir's footsteps south along the Diablo Range, over the Pacheco Pass, across the San Joaquin Valley, up the Sierra foothills, and then down into Yosemite Valley. And we hope you will take time to explore this part of California as Muir did, "drifting leisurely, paying very little compliance to roads or times," seeking out places of natural beauty, and viewing the world through Muir's eyes.

# JOHN MUIR'S
# STORY

DEAR FRIENDS,

Fate and flowers carried me to California, and I have reveled and luxuriated amid its mountains and plants and bright sky. I followed the Diablo foothills along the San Jose Valley to Gilroy, thence over the Diablo Mountains to the valley of San Joaquin by the Pacheco Pass, thence down the valley until about opposite the mouth of the Merced River, thence across the San Joaquin, and up into the Sierra Nevada, to the mammoth trees of Mariposa and the glorious Yosemite Valley, thence down the Merced to this place. No matter what direction I traveled, I waded in flowers by day and slept with them by night. Hundreds of

1

flowery gems, of most surpassing loveliness, touched my feet and buried them out of sight at every step. I was very happy, the larks and insects sang in streams of unmeasured joy, a sky of plants beneath me, and a sky of light above me, all kept by their Maker in perfect beauty and pure as heaven.

When I first set out [September 1867], on the long excursion that finally led me to California, I wandered afoot and alone, from Indiana to the Gulf of Mexico, with a plant press on my back, holding a generally southward course, like the birds when they are going from summer to winter. From the west coast of Florida I crossed the gulf to Cuba and enjoyed the rich tropical flora there for four happy weeks in January and February. I was intending to go thence to South America, get ashore anywhere on the north end of the continent, make my way through the woods to the headwaters of the Amazon, and float down that grand river to the ocean. But I was unable to find a ship bound for South America—fortunately perhaps, for I had incredibly little money for so long a trip, less than a hundred dollars, and had not yet fully recovered from a fever caught in the Florida swamps. Therefore I decided to postpone my South American trip and visit California for a year or two, to see its wonderful flora and the famous Yosemite Valley, the big trees and the vegetation in general. All the world was before me and every day was a holiday, so it did not seem important to which one of the world's wildernesses I first should wander.

My health, which suffered such wreck in the South, has been thoroughly patched and mended in the mountains of California. I came to life in the cool winds and crystal waters of the mountains. A month in the Sierra has affected a complete cure, and I am well again. Were it not for a thought, now and then, of loneliness and isolation, the pleasure of my existence would be complete. I have not received a single letter from anyone since my departure from Florida, and of course I am very lonesome and hunger terribly for the communion of friends. But I mean to settle here eight or nine months, and hope to see this big gap in tidings from friends well mended.

This is a splendid country, and one might truthfully make use of more than half of the Methodist hymn 'Land of pure delight' in describing it: it flows with more of milk and more of honey than ever did old Canaan in its happiest prime. Of all the bright shining ranks of happy days that God has given me since I left Wisconsin, these of California are the happiest.

# NEW YORK TO CALIFORNIA

I SAILED TO NEW YORK on a schooner loaded with oranges. On our arrival the captain, knowing something of the lightness of my purse, told me that I could continue to occupy my bed on the ship until I sailed for California,[1] getting my meals at a nearby restaurant. "This is the way we are all doing," he said. Consulting the newspapers, I found that the first ship sailed for Aspinwall in about ten days, and that the steerage passage to San Francisco by way of the isthmus was only forty dollars,[2] so took passage on the steamship *Santiago de Cuba*, sailing the next Thursday for Panama and then California's weeds and trees.[3]

The day before the sailing of the Panama ship [March 13, 1868] I bought a pocket map of California and allowed myself to be persuaded to buy a dozen large maps, mounted on rollers, with a map of the world on one side and the United States on the other.[4] In vain, I said I had no use for them. "But surely you want to make money in California, don't you? Everything out there is very dear. We'll sell you a dozen of these fine maps for two dollars each and you can easily sell them in California for ten dollars apiece." I foolishly allowed myself to be persuaded. The maps made a very large, awkward bundle, but fortunately it was the only baggage I had except my little plant press and a small India rubber bag.[5] I laid them in my berth in the steerage, for they were too large to be stolen and concealed.

The scenery of the ocean was intensely interesting, very far exceeding in beauty and magnificence the highest of my most ardent conceptions. There was a savage contrast between life in the steerage and my fine home on the little ship fruiter. Never before had I seen such a barbarous mob, especially at meals.

When the ship arrived at Aspinwall-Colón, I had half a day to ramble about and collect specimens before starting across the isthmus. I saw only a very little of the tropical grandeur of Panama, for my health was still in wreck, and I did not venture to wait for the arrival of another steamer. The isthmus train moved at cruel speed through the gorgeous Eden of vines and palms, and I could only gaze from the car platform, and weep and pray that the Lord would some day give me strength to see it better.

# San Francisco

AFTER A DELIGHTFUL SAIL among the scenery of the sea we reached San Francisco about the first of April.[6] I only stayed in San Francisco one day and then enquired of a man who was carrying carpenter's tools the nearest way out of town, to get to the uncultivated, wild part of the state. He in wonder asked, "But where do you want to go?" and I said, "Anywhere that is wild." This reply startled him. He seemed to fear I might be crazy and therefore the sooner I was out of town the better, so he directed me to the Oakland ferry and told me to cross the Bay there, and said that that would be as good a way out of town as any.

On the second day of April, 1868, I left San Francisco for Yosemite Valley,[7] companioned by a

young Englishman.[8] The orthodox route of "nearest and quickest" was by steam to Stockton, thence by stage to Coulterville or Mariposa, and the remainder of the way over the mountains on horseback.[9] But we had plenty of time, and proposed drifting leisurely mountainward, via the valley of San Jose, Pacheco Pass, and the plain of San Joaquin, and thence to Yosemite by any road that we chanced to find; enjoying the flowers and light, "camping out" in our blankets wherever overtaken by night, and paying very little compliance to roads or times. Accordingly, we crossed the Bay by the Oakland ferry, and leaving the train at East Oakland,[10] we took the first road we came to and proceeded up the valley of San Jose. The Oakland hills at this time, after a very rainy season, were covered with flowers[11]—patches of yellow and blue and white in endless variety—that made the slopes of the hills seem like a brilliant piece of patch-work.

# SANTA CLARA VALLEY

WE PROCEEDED UP the Santa Clara Valley to San Jose. It was the bloom-time of the year. The landscapes were fairly drenched with sunshine, all the air was quivering with the songs of the meadow-larks, and the hills were so covered with flowers that they seemed to be painted. Slow indeed was my progress through these glorious gardens, the first of the California flora I had seen. Cattle and cultivation were making few scars as yet, and I wandered enchanted in long wavering curves, knowing by my pocket map that Yosemite Valley lay to the east and that I should surely find it.

The valley of San Jose is one of the most fertile of the many small valleys of the Coast Ranges; its rich bottoms are filled with wheat fields and orchards and vineyards, and alfalfa meadows. It was now spring-time, and the weather was the best that we ever enjoyed. Larks and streams sang everywhere; the sky was cloudless, and the whole valley was a lake of light.

The atmosphere was spicy and exhilarating; my companion acknowledging over his national prejudices that it was the best he ever breathed—more deliciously fragrant than the hawthorn hedges of England. This San Jose sky was not simply pure and bright, and mixed with plenty of well-tempered sunshine, but it possessed a positive flavor—a taste that thrilled, from the lungs throughout every tissue of the body; every inspiration yielded a corresponding well-defined piece of pleasure that awakened thousands of new palates everywhere. Both my companion and myself had lived and dozed on common air for nearly thirty years, and never before this had discovered that our bodies contained such multitudes of palates or that this mortal flesh, so little valued by philosophers and teachers, was possessed of so vast a capacity for happiness.

We emerged from this ether baptism new creatures, born again; and truly not until this time were we fairly conscious that we were born at all. Never more, I thought, as we strode forward at faster speed, never more shall I sentimentalize about getting out of the mortal coil: this flesh is not a coil, it's a sponge steeped in immortality.

The last of the Coast Range foothills were in near view all the way to Gilroy; those of the Monte Diablo range on our left, those of Santa Cruz on our right. They were smooth and flowing, and their union with the valley was by curves and courses of most surpassing beauty. They were robed with the greenest grass and richest light I ever beheld, and were colored and shaded with myriads of flowers of every hue, which did not occur singly or in handfuls, scattered about in the grass, but grew close together, in smooth cloud-shaped companies, acres and hillsides in size, white, purple, and yellow, separate, yet blending to each other like the hills upon which they grew. Besides the white, purple, and yellow clouds, we occasionally saw a thicket of scarlet castilleias and silvery-leaved lupines, also splendid fields of wild oats (*Avena fatua*).[12] The delightful gilia (*G. tricolor*) was very abundant in sweeping hillside sheets, and a leptosiphon (*L. androsca*) and claytonias were everywhere by the roadsides, and lilies and dodecatheons by the streams: no wonder the air was so good, waving and rubbing on such a firmament of flowers!

Hundreds of crystal rills joined song with the

larks, filling all the valley with music like a sea, making it Eden from end to end. I tried to decide which of the plant-clouds was most fragrant: perhaps it was the white, composed mostly of a delicate boragewort; but doubtless all had a hand in balming the sky. Among trees we observed were the laurel (*Oreodaphne Californica*) and magnificent groves and tree-shaped groups of oaks, some specimens over seven feet in diameter; the white oaks (*Quercus lobata*) and (*Q. douglasii*), the black oak (*Q. sonomensis*), live oak (*Q. agrifolia*), together with several dwarfy species on the hills whose names we did not know. The prevailing north-west wind has permanently swayed all unsheltered trees up the valley; groves upon the more exposed hillsides lean forward like patches of lodged wheat. The Santa Cruz Mountains have grand forests of redwood (*Sequoia sempervirens*), some specimens near fifty feet in circumference.

# PACHECO PASS

PASSING THROUGH SAN JOSE and going on to Gilroy, I began to enquire the way to Yosemite and they said you had to cross the Coast Range through the Pacheco Pass, go over to the San Joaquin, and then enquire the way there. The goodness of the weather as we journeyed toward Pacheco was beyond all praise and description—fragrant, mellow, and bright. The sky was perfectly delicious, sweet enough for the breath of angels; every draught of it gave a separate and distinct piece of pleasure. I do not believe that Adam and Eve ever tasted better in their balmiest nook.

The Pacheco Pass was scarcely less enchanting than the valley. It resounded with crystal waters, and the loud shouts of thousands of California quails. In size these

about equal the eastern quail; not quite so plump in form. The male has a tall, slender crest, wider at top than bottom, which he can hold straight up, or droop backward on his neck, or forward over his bill, at pleasure; and, instead of "Bob White," he shouts: "pe-check-a," bearing down with a stiff, obstinate emphasis on "check."

Through a considerable portion of the pass the road bends and mazes along the groves of a stream, or down in its pebbly bed, leading one, now deep in the shadows of dogwoods and alders, then out in the light, through dry chaparral, over green carex meadows banked with violets and ferns, and dry plantless flood-beds of gravel and sand. The scenery, too, and all of nature in the pass was fairly enchanting. We found strange and beautiful mountain ferns in abundance all through the pass—some far down in dark cañons, as the polypodium and rock-fern, or high on sunlit braes, as *Pelloea mucronata*. Also we observed the delicate gold-powdered *Gynmogramma triangularis*, and *Pelloea andromedoefolia*, and the maidenhair (*Adiantum chilense*), and the broad shouldered bracken (*Pteris aquilina*), which is everywhere; and an aspidium and cystopteris, and two or three others that I was not acquainted with. Also in this rich garden pass we gathered many fine grasses and carices, and brilliant penstemons, azure and scarlet, and mints and lilies, and scores of others, strangers to us. There were banks of blooming shrubs, and countless assemblies of flowers, beautiful and pure as ever enjoyed the sun or shade of a mountain home.

And oh! What streams were there! Beaming, glancing, each with music of its own, singing as they go, leaping and gliding in shadow and light, onward along their lovely changing pathways to the sea; and hills rise over hills, and mountains rise over mountains, heaving, waving, swelling, in most glorious, overpowering, unreadable majesty.

After we were fairly over the summit of the pass, and had reached an open hill-brow, a scene of peerless grandeur burst suddenly upon us. At our feet, basking in sungold, lay the great Central Plain of California, bounded by the mountains on which we stood, and by the lofty, snow-capped Sierra Nevada; all in grandest simplicity, clear and bright as a new outspread map. Looking down from a height of fifteen hundred feet, extending north and south as far as I could see, lay a vast flower garden, smooth and level like a lake of gold— the floweriest part of the world I had yet seen. From the eastern margin of the golden plain arose the white Sierra; at the base ran a belt of gently sloping purplish foothills lightly dotted with oaks, above that a broad dark zone of coniferous forests, and above this forest zone arose the lofty mountain peaks, clad in snow. The atmosphere was so clear that the nearest of the mountain peaks, on the axis of the range, at a distance of more than one hundred and fifty miles, seemed to be at just the right distance to be seen broadly in their relations to one another, marshaled in glorious ranks and groups. It seemed impossible for a man to walk across the open folds without being seen, even at this distance. Perhaps more than three hundred miles of the range was comprehended in this one view.

The mighty Sierra, miles in height, and so gloriously colored and so radiant, seemed not clothed with light, but wholly composed of it, like the wall of some celestial city. Along the top and extending a good way down, was a rich pearl-gray belt of snow; below it a belt of blue and dark purple, marking the extension of the forests; and stretching along the base of the range a broad belt of rose-purple; all these colors, from the blue sky to the yellow valley, smoothly blending as they do in a rainbow, making a wall of light ineffably fine. Then it seemed to me that the Sierra should be called, not the Nevada or Snowy Range, but the Range of Light.

# SAN JOAQUIN VALLEY

IN HALF A DAY WE WERE DOWN over all the foothills, past the San Luis Gonzaga Ranch, and wading out in the grand level ocean of flowers. This plain, watered by the San Joaquin and Sacramento rivers, formed one flowerbed nearly four hundred miles in length by thirty in width—a smooth sea, ruffled a little in the middle by the trees fringing the river, and here and there by smaller cross streams from the mountains. One can scarce believe that these vast assemblies of flower families are permanent but rather that, actuated by some great special plant purpose, they have convened from every plain and mountain and meadow of their kingdom, and that each different coloring marked the boundaries of the various tribe and family encampments.

Florida is indeed a land of flowers, but for every single flower-creature that dwells in that most delightsome place, more than a hundred are living here. Here, here is Florida![13] Here flowers are not sprinkled apart with grass between as on our prairies, but grasses are sprinkled among the flowers; not as in Cuba, flowers piled upon flowers, heaped and gathered into deep glowing masses, but flowers side by side, raceme to raceme, petal to petal, touching but not entwined, branches weaving past and past each other but free and separate—one level sheet. True, in looking at this flower robe more closely it would seem to be thrice folded, mosses next to the ground, petaled flowers above them, grasses over all; but to our eyes they are one.

Crossing this greatest of flower gardens, and then the San Joaquin River at Hills Ferry, I drifted separate for many days[14] in this botanist's better land,[15] the largest days of my life, resting at times from the blessed plants in showers of bugs and sun-born butterflies; or I watched the smooth-bounding antelopes, or startled hares, skimming light and swift as eagles' shadows; or turning from all this fervid life, contemplating the Sierra, that mighty wall uprising from the brink of this lake of gold, miles in the higher blue, bearing aloft its domes and spires in spotless white, unshining and beamless, yet pure as pearl, clear and undimmed as the flowers at my feet. Never were mortal eyes more thronged with beauty.

The yellow of the *Compositae* is pure, deep, bossy solar gold, as if the sun had filled their rays and flowerets with the undiluted substance of his very self. In depth, the purple stratum was about ten or twelve inches; the yellow, seven or eight, and the moss stratum, of greenish yellow, one inch. But the purple stratum is dilute and transparent, so that the lower yellow is hardly dimmed; and only when a horizontal view is taken, so as to look edgewise through the upper stratum, does its color predominate. Therefore, when one stands on a wide level area, the gold immediately about him seems all in all; but on gradually looking wider the gold dims, and purple predominates. Out of sight is another stratum of purple, the ground forests of mosses, with purple stems, and purple cups. The color-beauty of these mosses, at least in the mass, was not made for human eyes, nor for the wild horses that inhabit these plains, nor the antelopes, but perhaps the little creatures enjoy their own beauty, and perhaps the insects that dwell in these forests and climb their shining columns enjoy it, but we know that however faint, and however shaded, no part of it is lost, for all color is received into the eyes of God.

When I walked, more than a hundred flowers touched my feet, at every step closing above them, as if wading in water. Go where I would, east or west, north or south, I still plashed and rippled in flower-gems; and at night I lay between two skies of silver and gold, spanned by a milky-way of vegetable suns. But all this beauty of life is fading year by year, fading like the glow of a sunset, foundering in the grossness of modern refinement. As larks are gathered in sackfuls, ruffled and blood-stained, to toy morbid appetite in barbarous towns, so is flower-gold gathered to slaughter pens in misbegotten carcasses of oxen and sheep. So always perish the plant peoples of temperate regions—feeble, unarmed, unconfederate, they are easily overthrown, leaving their lands to man and his few enslavable beasts and grasses. But vigorous flower nations of the South, armed and combined, hold plantfully their rightful kingdom; and woe to the lordly biped trespassing in these tropic gardens; catbriers seam his flesh, and saw-palmettoes grate his bones, and bayonets glide to his joints and marrow. But, alas! only one plant of this plain is armed; a tall purple mint, speared and lanced like a thistle. The weapons of plants are believed by some to be a consequence of "man's first disobedience." Would that all the flowers of the Sacramento and San Joaquin, were "cursed," thorned and thistled in safety!

# BOTANICAL
# INFORMATION

IN ORDER THAT some definite conception may be formed of the richness of this flower-field, I will give a harvest gathered by me from one square yard of plain, opposite Hills Ferry, a few miles from the Coast Range foothills, and taken at random, like a cupful of water from a lake. An approximation was made to the number of grass flowers by counting the panicles, to the flowers of the *Compositae* by counting the heads. The mosses were roughly estimated by counting the number growing on one square inch. All the flowers of the other natural orders were counted one by one.

LUPINE

GOLDFIELDS

MONKEY FLOWER

| NATURAL ORDER | NUMBER OF FLOWERS | NUMBER OF SPECIES |
|---|---|---|
| Graminaceae | 29,830 | 3 (1,000 panicles, 700 stems) |
| Compositae | 132,125 | 2 yellow (3,305 heads) |
| Leguminosae | 2,620 | 2 purple & white |
| Umbelliferae | 620 | 1 yellow |
| Polemoniaceae | 401 | 2 purple |
| Scrophulariaceae | 169 | 1 purple |
| Rubiaceae | 40 | 1 white |
| Geraniaceae | 22 | 1 purple |
| Unknown | 85 | 1 |
| Unknown | 60 | (plants unflowered, yellow) |
| Musci [mosses] | 1,000,000 | 2 purple (Funaria & Dicranum) |

TOTAL NUMBER OF NATURAL ORDERS:  9 TO 11

TOTAL NUMBER OF SPECIES:  16 TO 17

TOTAL NUMBER OF OPEN FLOWERS:  165,912

TOTAL NUMBER OF MOSSES:  1,000,000

In the above estimate, only open living flowers were taken into account. Those which were still in bud, together with those that were past flower, would number nearly as many more. The heads of the *Compositae* are usually regarded as one flower. Even then we would have seven thousand two hundred and sixty-two flowers, together with a thousand silky, transparent panicles of grasses, and a floor an inch thick of hooded mosses. The grasses have scarce any eaves, and do not interfere with the light of the other flowers, or with their color, in any marked degree.

February and March are the ripe springtime of the plain, April the summer, and May the autumn. The first beginnings of spring are controlled by the rains, which generally appear in December. Rains between May and December are very rare. This is the winter, a winter of drought and heat. But in no part of the year is plant-life wholly awanting. A few lilies with bulbs very deep in the soil, and a rosy compound called tarweed, and a species of erigonum, are slender, inconspicuous links, which continue the floral chain from season to season, around the year.

# FOOTHILLS

I HAD A WEEK OR TWO of fever before leaving the plains for Yosemite, but it was not severe, I was only laid up three or four days, and ere we were ready to recommence our march to Yosemite, May was about half done. On this part of my journey I was joined by a young Englishman, by the name of Chilwell, a most amusing companion, and we had several accidents and adventures.[16] We followed the Merced River, which I knew drained Yosemite Valley, and ascended the foothills from Snelling by way of Coulterville.

The flowers and grasses, so late in the pomp and power of full bloom, were dead, and their parched leaves crisped and crackled beneath our feet, as if they had literally been "cast into the oven." They were not given weeks and months to grow old; but they aged and died ere they could fade, standing side by side, erect and undecayed, bearing seed-cells and urns beautiful as corollas. After riding for two days in this autumn, we found summer again in the higher Sierra foothills. Flowers were spread confidingly open, the grasses waved their branches all bright and gay in the colors of healthy prime, and the winds and streams were cool. Above Coulterville, forty or fifty miles farther in the mountains, we came to spring. The leaves of the mountain-oaks were small and drooping, and still wore their first tintings of crimson and purple; and the wrinkles of their bud-folds were still distinct, as if newly opened; and, scattered over banks and sunny, mild sloping places, thousands of gentle mountain flowers were tasting life for the first time.

At the little mining town of Coulterville we bought flour and tea and made inquiries about roads and trails, and the forests we would have to pass through. The storekeeper, an Italian, took kindly pains to tell the pair of wandering wayfarers, new arrived in California, that the winter had been very severe, that in some places the Yosemite trail was still buried in snow eight or ten feet deep, and therefore we would have to wait at least a month before we could possibly get into the great Valley, for we would surely get lost should we attempt to go on. As to the forests, the trees, he said, were very large; some of the pines eight or ten feet in diameter.

In reply I told him that it would be delightful to see snow ten feet deep and trees ten feet thick, even if lost, but I never got lost in wild woods. "Well," said he, "go, if you must, but I have warned you; and anyhow you must have a gun, for there are bears in the mountains, but you must not shoot at them unless they come for you and are very, very close up." So at last, at Mr. Chilwell's anxious suggestion, we bought an old army musket with a few pounds of quail shot and large buckshot, good, as the merchant assured us, for either birds or bears.

A passable carriage road reached about twelve miles beyond Coulterville; the rest of the distance to the Valley was crossed only by a narrow trail. Our bill of fare in our camps was simple: tea and cakes, the latter toasted on the coals, made from flour without any leaven. Chilwell, being an Englishman, loudly lamented being compelled to live on flour and water, as he expressed it, and hungered for flesh. Therefore he made desperate efforts to shoot something to eat: quail and grouse, etc., but he was invariably unsuccessful, a poor shot, and declared the gun was of no use. I told him I thought that it was a good gun, if properly loaded and properly aimed, and that at the first camp we made I would show him how to load the gun and how to shoot.

At a height of one thousand feet or so we found many of the lily family blooming in all their glory, the *Calochortus* especially, a charming genus like European tulips, but finer, and many species of two new shrubs—especially *Ceanothus* and *Adenostoma*. The oaks, beautiful trees with blue foliage and white bark, forming open groves, gave a fine park-like effect. Higher, we met the first of the pines, with long gray foliage, large stout cones, and wide-spreading heads like palms. Then yellow pines, growing gradually more abundant as we ascended.

At Bower Cave, on the north fork of the Merced River, the streams were fringed with willows and azalea, ferns, flowering dogwood, etc. Here, too, we enjoyed the strange beauty of the cave in a limestone hill. At Deer Flat the wagon road ended in a trail, which we traced up the side of the dividing ridge parallel to the Merced and Tuolumne. A few miles farther "onward and upward," on the Pilot Peak ridge, we came again to the edge of winter. Scarce a grass or growing leaf was to be seen. The last of the lilies and spring violets were left far below; the winter scales were still wrapt close upon the buds of the dwarf oaks and alders. The great sugar pines waved their long arms solemnly, to the cold, loud, winds among rushing, changing, stormclouds. The sky became darker and more terrible. Many-voiced mountain winds swept the pines, speaking the dread language of the cold north. Snow began to fall thick and blinding, and soon my horse was deep in snow.[17] Thus, in less than a week from the hot autumn of the San Joaquin, we were struggling in a bewildering storm of mountain winter.

Fortunately, we reached Crane Flat, where some mountaineer had tried to establish a claim to the flat by building a little cabin of sugar pine shakes. Though we had arrived early in the afternoon I decided to camp there for the night, as the trail was buried in the snow that was about six feet deep. I wanted to examine the topography and plan our course. This was on or about May 20, at an elevation of six thousand one hundred and thirty feet. Chilwell cleared away the snow from the door and floor of the cabin, and made a bed of boughs from the fernlike silver fir, though I urged the same sort of bed made under the trees on the snow. But he had the house habit.

Here for the first time I saw the giants of the Sierra woods in all their glory. The forest was magnificent, composed in part of sugar pine (*Pinus lambertiana*), which is the king of all pines. Many specimens were over two hundred feet in height, eight to ten feet in diameter, fresh and sound as the sun which made them. The yellow pine (*Pinus ponderosa*) also grew there, and the cedar (*Libocedrus decurrens*); but the bulk of the forest was made up of the two silver firs (*Picea grandis* and *Picea amabilis*), the former always greatly predominating at that altitude. The sugar pine seemed to me the priest of the woods, ever addressing the surrounding trees, and blessing them. I began eagerly to sketch the noblest specimens, trying to draw every leaf and branch.

Chilwell reminded me of my promise about the gun, hoping eagerly for improvement to our bill of fare, however slight. I loaded the gun, paced off thirty yards from the cabin, or shanty, and told Mr. Chilwell to pin a piece of paper on the wall and see if I could not put shot into it and prove the value of the gun. Accordingly Mr. Chilwell pinned a piece of an envelope on the wall and vanished around the corner of the shanty, calling out, "Fire away."

I supposed that he had gone way back of the cabin,

but instead he went inside of the cabin and stood up against the mark that he had himself placed on the wall; and as the shake wall of soft sugar pine was only about half an inch thick, the shot passed through it and into his shoulder. He came rushing out, crying in great concern that I had shot him. The weather being cold, he had on three coats and as many shirts, and one of the coats was a heavy English overcoat. I discovered that the shot had passed through all this clothing and the pellets were imbedded beneath the skin and had to be picked out with the point of a pen knife. I said: "Why did you stand against that mark?" He said: "Well, I never thought that the shot would go through the 'ouse."

Leaving Crane Flat, we found our way easily enough over the deep snow, guided by the topography, holding a general easterly direction, getting, now and then, from the top of some headland, a glimpse of the Merced Cañon, which was my main guide. We discovered the trail on the brow of the Valley, just as the Bridal Veil came in sight. I didn't know that it was one of the famous falls I had read about, and, calling Chilwell's attention to it, I said, "See that dainty little fall over there. I should like to camp at the foot of it to see the ferns and lilies that may be there. It looks small from here, only about fifteen or twenty feet, but it may be sixty or seventy." So little did we then know of Yosemite magnitudes!

Descending these higher mountains toward the Merced, the snow gradually disappeared, tender leaves unfolded less and less doubtfully, violets and lilies appeared about us once more, and at length, arriving in the glorious Yosemite, we found it full of summer and spring. Thus, as colors blend in a rainbow, and as mountains curve to a plain, so meet and blend the plants and seasons of this delightsome land.

# YOSEMITE

THERE IS A KIND OF HOTEL in the Valley, but it is incomparably better to choose your own camp among the rocks and waterfalls. And of course we shunned the hotel in the Valley, seldom indulging even in crackers, both being too costly. After spending eight or ten days in visiting the falls and the high points of view around the walls, making sketches, collecting flowers and ferns, etc., we decided to make the return trip by the Mariposa trail to see the celebrated grove of giant sequoias, by way of Wawona, then owned by Galen Clark, the Yosemite pioneer.

The night before the start was made on the return trip, we camped near the Bridal Veil Meadows, where, as we lay eating our suppers by the light of the campfire, we were visited by a bear.[18] We heard him approaching by the heavy crackling of twigs. Chilwell, in alarm, after listening a while, said, "I see it! I see it! It's a bear, a grizzly! Where is the gun? You take the gun and shoot him—you can shoot best." (I had shot him, you know.) But the gun had only a charge of birdshot in it; therefore, while the bear stood on the opposite side of the fire, at a distance of probably twenty-five or thirty feet, I hastily loaded in a lot of buckshot. The buckshot was too large to chamber and therefore it made a zigzag charge on top of the birdshot charge, the two charges occupying about half of the barrel. Thus armed, the gun held at rest, pointed at the bear, we sat hushed and motionless, according to instructions from the man who sold the gun, solemnly waiting and watching, as full of fear as the musket of shot. Finally, after sniffing and whining for his supper what seemed to us a long time, the young inexperienced beast walked off. We were much afraid of his returning to attack us. We did not then know that bears never attack sleeping campers, and dreading another visit, we kept awake, on guard, most of the night.

# Mariposa Grove to Hopeton

LIKE THE COULTERVILLE TRAIL, all the high-lying part of the Mariposa trail was deeply snow-buried, but we found our way, without any tracks to guide us, without the slightest trouble, steering by the topography, in a general way, along the brow of the canyon of the south fork of the Merced River, and in a day or two reached Wawona. Here we replenished our little flour sack and Mr. Clark gave us a piece of bear meat. We then pushed eagerly on up the Wawona ridge through a magnificent sugar pine forest and into the far-famed Mariposa sequoia grove. The sun was down when we entered the grove, but we soon had a good fire and at supper that night we tasted bear meat for the first time. My flesh-hungry companion ate it eagerly, though to me it seemed so rank and oily that I was unable to swallow a single morsel.

After supper we replenished the fire and gazed enchanted at the vividly illumined brown boles of the giants towering about us, while the stars sparkled in wonderful beauty above their huge domed heads. We camped here long uncounted days, wandering about from tree to tree, taking no note of time. The longer we gazed, the more we admired not only their colossal size, but their majestic beauty and dignity. Greatest of trees, greatest of living things, their noble domes, poised in unchanging repose, seemed to belong to the sky, while the great firs and pines about them looked like mere latter-day saplings, like mere weeds growing among corn, so much was their grandeur dwarfed by these sequoia giants.

While we camped in the Mariposa Grove, the abundance of bear tracks caused Mr. Chilwell no little alarm, and he proposed that we load the gun properly with buckshot and without any useless birdshot; but there was no means of drawing the charge. It had to be shot off. The recoil was so great that it bruised his shoulder and sent him spinning like a top. Casting down the miserable gun, kicking the bad luck musket among the sequoia cones and branches that littered

the ground, he stripped and examined his unfortunate shoulder. In painful indignation and wrath, he found it black and blue and more seriously hurt by the bruising recoil blow than by the shot at Crane Flat.

When we got down to the hot San Joaquin plain at Snelling, the grain fields were nearly ready for the reaper, and we began to enquire for a job to replenish our remaining stock of money, which was now very small—though we had not spent much; the grand royal trip of more than a month in the Yosemite region having cost us only about three dollars each.[19]

Looking back on what I have written I see that it is nothing—just nothing, and it will not carry you a drop, not a drop, my friends, from all these oceans and gulfs and bays of plant loveliness. Can you not come? Just come and see what you can make of these great lessons of mountain and plain. Yosemite alone is worth the expense and danger of any journey in the world. It is by far the grandest of all of the special temples of Nature I was ever permitted to enter. It must be the sanctum sanctorum of the Sierra, and I trust that you will all be led to it.

*John Muir*
*July 1868*
*Nr. Hopeton*

# Notes

INTRODUCTION

1. By 2006, the little dirt roads Muir had followed in 1868 were mostly paved roads, busy city streets, or highways. So, just as Muir did not follow the expected route to Yosemite, we did not follow his exact footsteps. Instead, we walked a parallel route following the Bay Trail, public right-of-ways, bike trails, and nature trails, passing through as many city, county, state, and national parks and open spaces as possible. Our goal was to find the urban wilderness and see California through Muir's eyes. For specific details of the trip, see our book, *Muir Ramble Route* (Madera, CA: Poetic Matrix Press, 2010).

JOHN MUIR'S STORY

1. The First Transcontinental Railroad was not completed until 1869.

2. In 1868, there was a fare war between steamer lines. First-class fares dropped from $450 in 1867 to $150 in 1868. Muir says his steerage-class ticket was about $40. (John Olmsted, a contemporary traveler to California, wrote in his book *A Trip to California in 1868* [New York: Trow's Printing and Bookbinding, 1880], that a steerage ticket cost $45.)

3. As editor William Frederic Badè explains in Muir's book *A Thousand-Mile Walk to the Gulf* (Boston: Houghton Mifflin, 1913), the *Nebraska* had left for her maiden voyage around Cape Horn in January of 1868. Muir took the *Santiago de Cuba* to Aspinwall-Colón on the east coast of Panama, crossed Panama by train, and then took the northward-bound *Nebraska* to San Francisco.

4. A "pocket map" is a small folding map. It is likely Muir had either Bancroft's "Map of California, Nevada, Utah, and Arizona" (San Francisco: H. H. Bancroft, 1864 or 1868) or "A New Map of the States of California and Nevada" by Leander Ransom and A. J. Doolittle (San Francisco: W. Holt, 1867). Both maps show mountain ranges, rivers, cities, and major roads, but neither map has the detailed information of a modern street or topographic map, nor do they show a route from Pacheco Pass to Yosemite via Hills Ferry.

5. Muir used the plant press to preserve botanical samples. It was about twelve by eighteen inches and made with strips of a strong, stable wood (like white oak) nailed together in a lattice pattern. In Muir's day, botanists used straw board

and newspaper in place of today's corrugated cardboard and blotters. Muir once wrote a letter to his sister on narrow strips of newspaper, saying he had forgotten his writing paper and was using paper torn from the empty margins of the paper in his plant press. Muir's India rubber bag was the 1868 version of a dry bag/backpack. It was made out of rubber, or latex, from India, which at the time was commonly used for waterproofing.

6. The March 28, 1868, issue of the *Alta California* has an article announcing that the *Nebraska* had arrived the previous evening. The article contains a passenger list with over 120 specific names, then ends with "and 259 others." Muir was one of those 259 others.

7. It is not certain when Muir actually started his trip. He usually says he arrived in San Francisco on or about the first of April, spent one day in the city, and left the next day, giving the date as April 2. If he actually arrived March 28, a Saturday, could he have sold the large maps bought in New York that day or the next, or would he have had to wait until Monday, March 30, or even longer, before he would have been ready to leave?

8. In the 1872 magazine article "Rambles of a Botanist Among the Plants and Climates of California" (*Old and New*, June 1872), Muir never names this young Englishman. However, in his 1907 Pelican Bay manuscript (unpublished), Muir mentions a "young Englishman by the name of Chilwell" (page 29) and also calls him a "cockney." Since this describes a point later on in his journey, it might imply that his earlier English companion was a different person. The Pelican Bay manuscript reference is also the first time the name Chilwell is used. (See also notes 14 and 16.)

9. In 1868, the most common route from San Francisco to Yosemite was by ferry from San Francisco to Stockton, by stage from Stockton to Coulterville, and then by horse from Coulterville into the Yosemite Valley. Muir took a different route, but it was one that had been used regularly since the days of the forty-niners to reach the "southern mines" of Mariposa County. Our study of maps from the late 1800s showed Muir did not have many roads to choose from. For example, there were only two roads leading south out of Oakland. One was the old mission road, traversing the foothills of the Oakland hills; the other was a road used to access the landings for shipping on San Francisco Bay. These two roads merged together near present-day Milpitas. They then became the Oakland Road, which ended at the northeastern boundary of the then small city of San Jose.

10. In 1868, the San Francisco and Oakland Railroad ran ferry service between the two cities. The bay was shallow on the Oakland side. To ensure uninterrupted service regardless of the tide, in 1863 the railroad had constructed a wharf three-quarters-of a mile long. Passengers got off the ferry on the wharf, then hopped on a train that took them into Oakland. There was a West Oakland station near

the terminus of the wharf, and standard service was provided to a station at Seventh Street and Broadway. In 1868, train service extended as far southeast as Hayward (soon to be joined with the Central Pacific's transcontinental terminus in Sacramento). But, as Muir states, he left the train in East Oakland, as service farther would have cost extra money. So, we assume Muir began his walk at Seventh and Broadway.

11. The winter of 1867–1868 was the fourth rainiest year on record for San Francisco, with a total of 38.84 inches for the season. Most of the rain fell in December and January. It even snowed in San Francisco in January. Records in the National Archives in San Bruno, California, show it rained lightly on April 3 and 7, heavily from April 9 to 12, lightly from April 13 to 15, and then did not rain again until May 13, when only one hundredth of an inch fell.

The winter of 2006, when we took our first trip on the Muir Ramble Route, had similar heavy rainfall, with a total of 38.4 inches. It also rained the first two weeks of April, and there was snow in San Francisco in January.

12. Some of the names Muir uses to describe plants differ from those used today. We have not changed Muir's text in this regard. Common names for plants have always varied, and the botanical names for some plants have changed since Muir's time to reflect new scientific understandings.

13. We understand this to mean that if "Florida" is the name one should give to a place that is "the land of flowers," then the San Joaquin Valley should be called Florida.

14. This account indicates that Muir separated from his English companion for a while, after crossing the river at Hills Ferry. At the time, Hills Ferry was a rough-and-tumble San Joaquin River port town filled with bars and brothels. In "Rambles of a Botanist," Muir implies that the two companions eventually rejoined, stating, "Ere we were ready to recommence our trip…" (See also notes 8 and 16.)

15. Inspired by this visit, John Muir's first act of conservation in California was to purchase land near Hills Ferry to try to protect it from development. In his article "The National Parks and Forest Reservations" (*Sierra Club Bulletin*, May 1896), Muir recounts, "I tried to save a quarter section of the flowery San Joaquin plain when it began to be plowed for farms; but this scheme also failed, as the fence around it could not be kept up without constant watching, night and day."

16. Muir's "Rambles of a Botanist" states that he and the Englishman left San Francisco together. In the Pelican Bay manuscript, this companion is not mentioned until after crossing the San Joaquin at Hills Ferry, when Muir writes, "This part of my journey, I was accompanied by a young Englishman by the name of Chilwell, a most amusing companion."

The first mention of Chilwell's first name is in T. H. Watkins's *John Muir's America* (New York: Crown Publishers, 1976). Watkins calls him Joseph Chilwell in a passage that is not footnoted. Subsequent writers followed Watkins's lead. In *Rediscovering America* (New York: Viking, 1985), Fredrick Turner also names the companion Joseph Chilwell. Turner footnotes this sentence, referring to an article by Melville B. Anderson ("The Conversation of John Muir," *American Museum Journal*, March 1915), but that article does not mention Chilwell. Later, in a footnote on page 375, Turner refers to a little marble-bound notebook Muir used on his passage to California through Panama as the source for his information. This book is in the Holt-Atherton Special Collections, and a thorough reading did not reveal a single reference to Chilwell.

Further attempts to learn more about Chilwell brought no conclusive results. The bulk of San Francisco's early port records were destroyed in the 1906 earthquake, and a search of New York port records for the 1860s list only one Chilwell, named William, who arrived August 26, 1867, on the ship *City of Antwerp*. That record states William was born in 1837, and though a year older than Muir, he could have been Muir's "young companion."

The 1880 California census includes another William Chilwell, born in England in 1846. At the time of the census, this Chilwell was partners with a Scot, Amos Campbell, in a sheepherding business in San Diego. The 1861 British census records also list a William Chilwell, born in 1846, the son of William and Elizabeth Hopkins of Newton, Leicestershire. If this was Muir's Chilwell, he would have been no "cockney"; but the circumstantial evidence of age, profession, and an association with Scottish sheepherders makes him a good candidate to be Muir's companion.

A study of British census records from 1841 to 1881 shows that Chilwell is an uncommon name with a very small geographical distribution, most coming from Warwickshire or nearby. Perhaps Muir was using the term "cockney" in a more generic sense to mean Englishman. The only record we found of a Chilwell with the given name Joseph was in the British 1891 census, and this one, listed as born in 1845 in Hermitage, Polesworth, Newmarket, London, could fit the description of "cockney," which was usually used to refer to people from London's East End. According to the census, Joseph Chilwell was a married chemist with four children. He was the right age to be Muir's companion, but we do not know if he had traveled to America. (See also notes 8 and 14.)

17. Muir rode a horse on his trip. The fact is verified in his May 16, 1869, letter to Mrs. Jeanne Carr, his friend and mentor from Wisconsin. Muir wrote: "Last May, I made the trip on horseback, going by Coulterville and returning by Mariposa. A passable carriage road reached about twelve miles beyond Coulterville; the rest of the distance to the Valley was crossed only by a narrow

trail." In 1868, most tourists hired a guide and rented a horse in Coulterville. Muir mentions purchasing supplies in Coulterville but does not make it clear if that is where he got the horse.

18. Much has changed since Muir first visited Yosemite. Guns are no longer allowed in the park, and there are no more grizzly bears in the area; but Yosemite is still home to several hundred American black bears. These bears have a voracious appetite, are incredibly curious, and have an amazing sense of smell. This combination tempts them to seek modern high-calorie food. Sometimes bears that routinely get our food become aggressive, and sometimes they have to be killed as a result. By storing your food properly, you can prevent a bear's unnecessary death.

19. This three dollars refers to the money Muir spent while in the Yosemite region, not on the whole trip, as it could not include the costs he incurred to rent a horse and buy a gun. In his May 1869 letter to Jeanne Carr, Muir writes: "Here is, I think, a fair estimate of the cost of the round trip from Stockton, allowing, say, ten days from time of departure from Mariposa till arrival at [the] same point. Stage fare and way expenses to and from Mariposa, say $40.00; saddle horse, $20.00; provisions, cooking utensils, etc., $15.00; total, direct expense for one person, $75.00. Each additional day spent in the Valley would cost about $3.00."

# Source Notes

Following are the sources for the text of John Muir's first trip to Yosemite, with the abbreviations we have assigned to them. Unless otherwise noted, Muir is the author of the source.

LAL: *The Life and Letters of John Muir*, edited by William Frederic Badè (Boston: Houghton Mifflin Co., 1924)

LTA: Letter to Ann Galloway (Muir's sister), August 1868

LTCF: Letter to Jeanne Carr (friend and mentor from Wisconsin), February 1869

LTCJ: Letter to Jeanne Carr, July 1868

LTCM: Letter to Jeanne Carr, May 1869

LTCN: Letter to Jeanne Carr, November 1868

LTD: Letter to David Muir (Muir's brother), March 1868

LTM: Letter to the Moore and Merrill families (friends from Indiana), July 1868

PBM: Pelican Bay manuscript: an unpublished, transcribed oral history dictated in 1907 near Pelican Bay, Klamath Lake, Oregon, and catalogued as "Autobiographical sketches: from leaving university to about 1906," ca. 1908, John Muir Papers, Holt-Atherton Special Collections, University of the Pacific Library. © 1984 Muir-Hanna Trust

ROB: "Rambles of a Botanist Among the Plants and Climates of California,"
      *Old and New* 5 (January–July 1872)
TMW: *A Thousand-Mile Walk to the Gulf*, edited by William Frederic Badè
      (Boston: Houghton Mifflin Co., 1916)
TNP: "The National Parks and Forest Reservations" (proceedings of the
      meeting of the Sierra Club held November 23, 1895), *Sierra Club Bulletin* 1,
      no. 6 (May 1896)
YOS: *The Yosemite* (New York: Century Company, 1912)

John Muir's quotes in the preface come from the following original source material:

"devote the rest of my life": LAL, page 155
"I decided to visit California": YOS, page 3
"Yo Semite alone is worth the expense": LTM
"drifting leisurely": ROB, page 767

Following is a list giving the original sources used to create the text of this volume's
"John Muir's Story." The first line of the referenced paragraph is followed by the
abbreviations of its sources. The primary source is given first, followed by the
secondary source, and so on.

Fate and flowers carried me to California: LTM, LTCJ, LTA
When I first set out: YOS, page 4
My health, which suffered such wreck in the South: LTD, LTM, LTCJ
This is a splendid country: LTD

New York to California
I sailed to New York on a schooner: TMW, page 185; LTD
The day before the sailing: TMW, page 186
The scenery of the ocean: TMW, page 186
When the ship arrived: TMW, page 186

San Francisco
After a delightful sail: TMW, page 188; LAL, page 178; PBM, page 258–59;
      YOS, page 4; LTCJ
On the second day of April, 1868: ROB, page 767; LAL, page 178; PBM,
      page 259

Santa Clara Valley
We proceeded up the Santa Clara Valley: LAL, page 179; YOS, page 4
The valley of San Jose: LAL, page 179
The atmosphere was spicy: LAL, page 179
We emerged from this ether baptism: ROB, page 768
The last of the Coast Range foothills: TMW, page 189; ROB, page 768
Hundreds of crystal rills: TMW, page 189; ROB, page 768

PACHECO PASS

Passing through San Jose: PBM, page 259; TMW, page 189

The Pacheco Pass was scarcely: LAL, page 180

Through a considerable portion: ROB, page 769; LAL, page 180; TMW, page 189

And oh! What streams: TMW, page 190

After we were fairly over: ROB, page 769; LAL, page 181

The mighty Sierra, miles in height: YOS, page 5

SAN JOAQUIN VALLEY

In half a day we were down: ROB, page 769; TMW, page 191

Florida is indeed a land of flowers: TMW, page 191; LTM

Crossing this greatest of flower gardens: ROB, page 770; PBM, page 261

The yellow of the *Compositae*: ROB, page 770; LAL, page 181; LTM

When I walked: ROB, page 770–71

BOTANICAL INFORMATION

In order that some definite conception: ROB, page 771; LTCJ; LTM

FOOTHILLS

I had a week or two of fever: PBM, page 262; LAL, page 182; LTD

The flowers and grasses: ROB, page 771; LTCN

At the little mining town: LAL, page 182

In reply I told him: LAL, page 183

A passable carriage road: LTCM; LAL, page 183

At a height of one thousand feet: LAL, page 183

At Bower Cave: LAL, page 184; ROB, page 771; LTCN

Fortunately, we reached Crane Flat: LAL, page 184; ROB, page 771

Here for the first time: TNP, page 282; ROB, page 772; YOS, page 99

Chilwell reminded me: PBM, pages 263–64; LAL, page 185

I supposed that he had gone: LAL, page 185

Leaving Crane Flat: LAL, page 185

Descending these higher mountains: ROB, page 772; LTCN

YOSEMITE

There is a kind of hotel: PBM, page 262; LAL, page 185; LTCM

The night before the start: PBM, page 265; LAL, page 185

MARIPOSA GROVE TO HOPETON

Like the Coulterville trail: LAL, page 186

After supper we replenished: LAL, page 187

While we camped in the Mariposa Grove: LAL, page 187

When we got down: LAL, page 188

Looking back on what I have written: LTM, LTCJ

YOSEMITE
CONSERVANCY.

yosemiteconservancy.org

Yosemite Conservancy inspires people to support projects and
programs that preserve Yosemite and enrich the visitor experience.

Library of Congress Control Number: 2017956271

Cover illustrations by Emily Brown
Design and colorization by Eric Ball Design

ISBN 978-1-930238-83-1

Printed in the USA by Jostens, Inc., represented by Qualibre, Inc.

1 2 3 4 5 6 – 22  21  20  19  18